LET'S
INVESTIGATE!

LET'S INVESTIGATE

MAKING YOUR OWN COSTUMES

Published in this edition by Peter Haddock Ltd, Pinfold Lane,
Bridlington, East Yorkshire YO16 5BT

ISBN 0 7105 0993 6

Printed and bound in India

PART ONE

FANCY DRESS IN MANY GUISES

Fancy dress covers not only costumes made for parties and fancy dress competitions but also costumes made for pageants, dance, play and opera productions.

It is, of course, possible to hire costumes from theatrical costumiers, but this is usually expensive and not always satisfactory if you want your individual costume, or a whole group, to have a particular style.

Various types of costume will be dealt with in the different sections of this book, but here are a few general suggestions.

Do not be too ambitious. You may wish to make a costume that represents a Klingon from Star Trek, or Queen Elizabeth I, but do consider the difficulties.

If you wish to represent a character from a book or from history, study, for the former any descriptions in the text and illustrations; for the latter, study portraits or photographs and books on the history of costume.

The fabrics used in the past were often different from those used today. Remember, early costumes were made of hand-woven cloth, so use woollens and linen for these. If possible, try to find fabrics that look like those of the particular period: printed chintz can suggest the 18th century, soft muslins the early 19th century and so on. To give the heavy quality that many period costumes have, mount the outer material on calico. If the costume is only to be used once, experiment with paper.

You can apply one fabric on another easily by using an iron-on interlining, such as Vilene, which is available in different thicknesses and sizes. You can 'fake' various trimmings and accessories. Dog chains make excellent 'chains of office'; dog collars, belts, rope and piping cord-gilded makes a rich braid; paperclips of the 'stud' variety give a metal studded look to a medieval tunic.

Large clear sequins painted white make good 'pearls'; all kinds of hardware goods, such as curtain rings and hooks, can make effective jewellery. Feather dusters will provide you with bright coloured feathers with which to trim Elizabethan or Edwardian hats.

In attempting mythical or fantastic costumes, be free in your interpretation. For example, if at Christmas you take part in Nativity or fairy tale plays, which call for angels or for fairies, the costumes for these parts may be interpreted in many ways.

The angels do not *necessarily* need large wings, which means constructing a kind of harness—a cape of feathers can more easily suggest wings.

Fairies do not necessarily have to be dressed in the traditional white net and tinsel, but can have tights covered in sequins, to suggest a flash of light, or they could have soft transparent cloaks to suggest a drift of mist.

If you are 'dressing' a play, *do* plan the costumes as a group. This is very important when dealing with the colour.

SOME HELPFUL ADVICE

You will need the help of an adult to create the costumes described in this book. Make sure that you have been shown the safe and correct way to handle sharp instruments and needles before you start, and, if you are not experienced witha sewing machine, ask an adult to machine-sew garments where instructed to do so.

You might not be familiar with some of the terms used in this book—have a look at this glossary before reading any further:

basque—a bodice that extends below the waist

bias binding—a strip of material used to bind hems, as an interfacing, or as decoration

bodice—a tight-fitting garment that extends from the shoulder to the waist

bone—a thin strip of plastic that is used to stiffen and shape garments

CB—abbreviation of centre back

CF—abbreviation of centre front

facing—a fabric used to finish the raw edges of a material, usually at the neck, armholes and sleeves

galloon—a narrow band of cord or braid used for decoration on clothes or furniture

gusset—a piece of material inserted into a garment to strengthen or enlarge it

interfacing or **interlining**—fabric used between certain points of a garment and the facings, such as the collar, lapels or hem line, to strengthen and shape them. Iron-on interfacings such as Vilene are appropriate for use with a wide variety of fabrics

pinking shears—dressmaking scissors with a serrated edge that are used to prevent fraying on the seams and raw edges of garments

RS—abbreviation of right side (of the material)

slipstitch—a very small neat stitch used to join two folded edges or a folded hem edge

tack—a temporary stitch used to hold together two or more fabric layers during the fitting and making-up stages

welt—a raised seam or edge on a knitted garment

WS—abbreviation of wrong side (of the material)

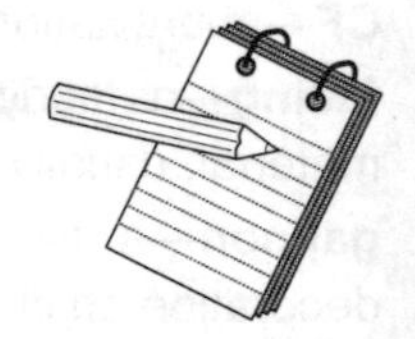

PART TWO

FOR THE BEGINNER

Here are a number of costumes that may be made fairly easily by collecting together ready-made garments owned by you, or by your family or friends, then adding a few bits and pieces that are easy to make or adapt.

These costumes are often based on characters from books—so you can look at the illustrations in the various books to help you in making the costumes. They are intended for fancy dress competitions or parties but, of course, if you are performing a dramatised version of the book they are also suitable for stage use.

Project

Be an Alice

Alice in Wonderland is suitable for girls aged 8 to 11 (*see* figure 1). You need the following:

A pink or a light blue cotton dress with tight bodice, a turned down collar, puff sleeves and a full gathered skirt. If you cannot arrange the tucks on the skirt, stitch on several rows of braid.

Several fairly stiff petticoats are needed to hold out the skirt of the dress.

A plain white cotton or organdie pinafore—it is possible to buy one similar to the illustration, probably

Figure 1: An Alice in Wonderland dress

adding the shoulder frills, or you can make one in cheap cotton organdie, following figure 2. The lines of stitching in the pinafore can be made by stitching on braid (bias binding or the plain type used to finish lampshades).

Flat black pumps, white tights and a white or pale blue headband will complete the costume.

Pinafore

Use a bodice pattern on which to base the upper part; trace out the bodice then draw a line from the shoulder to the waist (measuring on yourself to see how wide you want it at the waist). Cut the bodice part twice, machine the shoulder seams on both and press.

Place one bodice part on top of the other, right sides facing. Machine around neck and down the centre back. Trim the seams notching the neck turning. Turn to the right side and tack round the edge, rolling the seam flat, and press with an iron (*see* diagram 1 of figure 2).

Cut the 'wing' parts as illustrated, allowing one-and-a-half times the length you require for gathering. Turn in the outer edge 5 millimetres (1/4 inch) and fold again, making a 1.5-centimetre (1/2-inch) hem; tack and machine. Machine the bias binding or braid on the 'wings' as shown. Turn in the outer edge of the bodice parts about 1.5 centimetres (1/2 inch); slip the 'wing' parts in between the bodice part; tack all three pieces together and machine close to the edge (*see* diagram 2 of figure 2).

Machine the bias binding to the bodice parts as shown in the sketch. Cut a strip of fabric for the waistband 5 centimetres (2 inches) wide, plus seams by your waist measurement, and 90 centimetres (36 inches) for the bow. With the right side inside, machine across the ends and along from each end, leaving an

Figure 2: The illustrations show you how you go about making your own pinafore

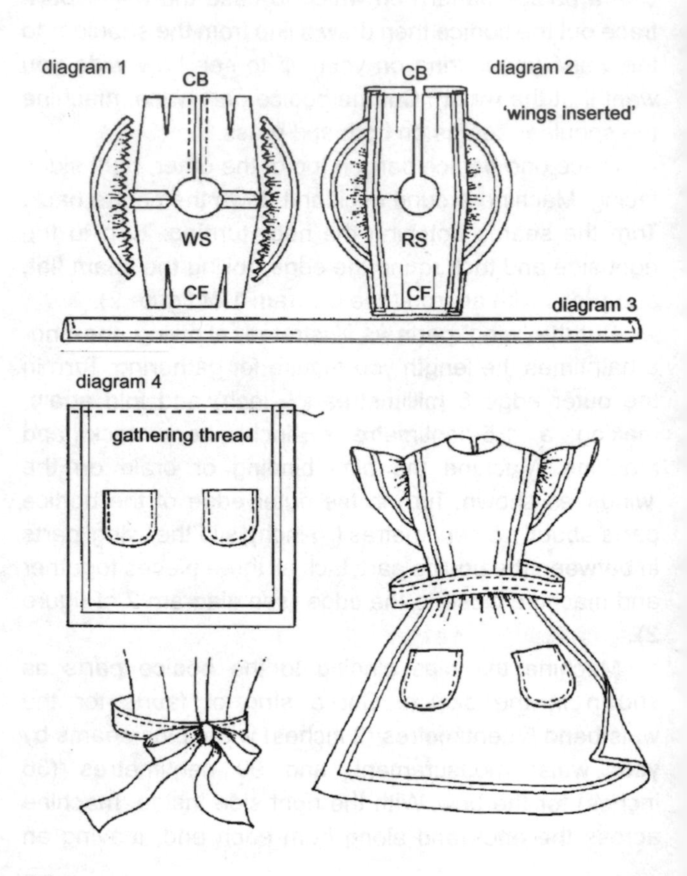

opening a little bigger than the width of the front bodice part (*see* diagram 3 of figure 2). Snip across the corners and trim the seams; turn to the right side, then tack the edge and press. Cut the skirt part double the width of the first bodice part at the waist, by the length you require. Machine hem the edges and attach bias binding or braid.

Before you cut the pockets, make a pattern in paper. Turn in the edges of the pockets and press. Machine to the skirt part of the apron. Run a gathering thread along the top of the skirt part (*see* diagram 4 of figure 2). Turn in each side of the waistband on the unjoined edge. Insert this into skirt part and tack all three pieces together.

Try on your apron, and pin the back bodice part to the waistband, leaving room to tie the bow at the centre of the back. Machine across the lower edge of the waistband, catching in the skirt part. Machine the bodice parts to the waistband. Fasten the back neck with a hook and eye.

Project

Make a Mad Hatter

The Mad Hatter is suitable for boys or girls aged 8 to 11 (*see* figure 3). You can make the costume for this character from *Alice in Wonderland* by using an old dark blue or grey blazer, a waistcoat in a neutral colour and jeans. You need to make a collar and tie and a top hat.

For the jacket, remove the collar of the blazer or old

Figure 3: The Mad Hatter—an old blazer, waistcoat and jeans are the basis for making this Mad Hatter's outfit

jacket and re-neaten the edge by turning one edge in on the other and hemming. Fold the lapels forward and press out the previous fold line; fasten with a large hook at the neck.

Try to get hold of an old waistcoat and adjust the seams to allow it to fit. The length may be reduced by 'lifting' the garment at the shoulder seams, and the width by taking in the side seams. If the length is still too long, cut to the required length, allowing for a turning, then turn in this allowance and make a turned-up hem.

For the trousers, mark out the checks with chalk, then cut out squares of white fabric—felt would be best; iron these onto Vilene; strip off the Vilene backing and iron the checks on to the marked position on the jeans. To strengthen, hem round each square.

Cut out the collar in white cotton. Use a heavy interlining to stiffen and just stitch by hand or machine around the edge. The collar may be attached to the collar of the jacket. For the bow, use cotton, and paint or appliqué (using Vilene) the large spots in blue or red; tie a bow and stitch it in position. Stitch it to wide elastic to go around your neck; this can be closed with a press fastener.

Make a top hat from card (*see* figure 4). Paint the whole black or grey, and finish with a ribbon band and the price card as illustrated. The costume is completed with a pair of blue striped socks and black plimsolls.

Figure 4: The Mad Hatter's Top Hat

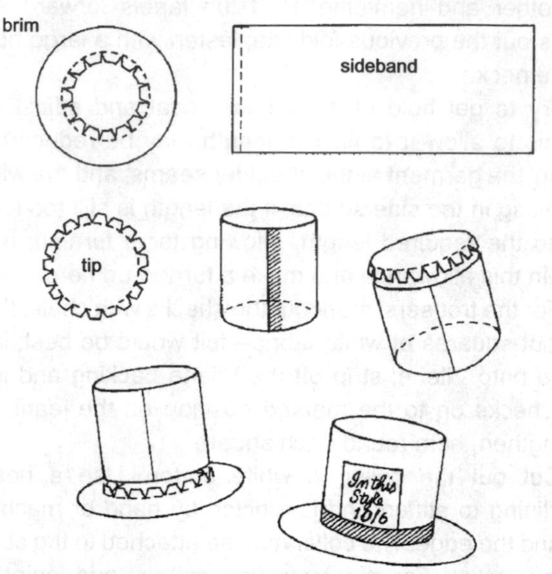

Draw a circle in card, using a plate as a guide to fit your head, then draw beyond this the outer edge of the brim about 10 centimetres (4 inches). Cut the sideband of the hat about 20–25 centimetres (9–11 inches) high by the head measurement (inner edge of the brim) to allow for an overlap. Cut the circle for the top of the hat (tip) the same size as the inner section of the brim, allowing a turn of 10 millimetres (½ inch). To make up, join the ends of the sideband, forming a tube, with Sellotape or stick with glue. Snip the 'tip' as indicated and slide it into the top of the sideband, then stick in place. Snip the brim and slide this section up under the sideband, sticking it in place.

Be Mary Poppins

Mary Poppins is suitable for girls aged 8-16 (*see* figure 5). To wear this costume, according to the story, you should have dark hair that must be drawn up into a 'bun' on the top of your head.

Begin with the coat. An old gaberdine raincoat in dark blue would be ideal. The skirt should be made of denim (either pink or blue) and appliquéd with white stripes.

The long white scarf should be tied quite tightly at the neck and appliquéd with stripes to match the colour of the denim skirt. The 'sailor' hat should be trimmed with artificial flowers, again in the same colour as the skirt. You may be able to borrow a hat of this type in straw, but if not it can be made of card in the same way as the hat for the Mad Hatter. Attach elastic to hold it on.

The strapped shoes, the tights and the umbrella should all be black. The handle of the umbrella should be shaped like a parrot's head (*see* figure 6). Dark blue gloves, with long cuffs if possible, and a large bag will complete the outfit.

Project

Be Oliver Twist

For this costume you will need to find a jacket that you have grown out of so that the sleeves are short and it is very tight. Cut it off at waist level, and re-neaten the edge

Figure 5: A Mary Poppins costume

by 'turning in' the outer fabric, and hemming with a slipstitch; press and then turn in the lining; hem it down. The jacket should be dark grey, navy or black.

Try to find an old pair of grey trousers which will be tight and short. For this costume they should be fastened

Figure 6: Shaping the handle of Mary Poppins' umbrella like a parrot's head

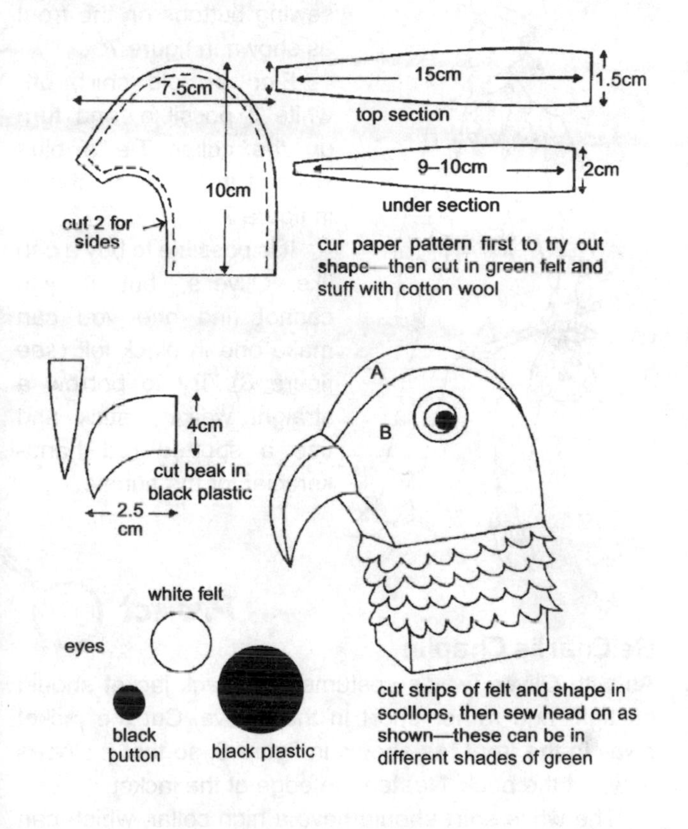

Figure 7: Oliver Twist

with a flap at the front. You can achieve this effect by sewing buttons on the front as shown in figure 7.

Find an old shirt, off-white if possible, and turn up the collar. Tie a blue scarf at the neck as shown in figure 7.

It is possible to buy a cap like Oliver's, but if you cannot find one you can make one in black felt (*see* figure 8). Try to borrow a straight walking stick and use a spotted red handkerchief for the bundle.

Project

Be Charlie Chaplin

As with Oliver Twist's costume, the black jacket should be tight and rather short in the sleeve. Cut the jacket away in the front, as shown in figure 9, so that it slopes down at the back. Neaten the edge of the jacket.

The white shirt should have a high collar, which can

Figure 8: Oliver Twist's cap

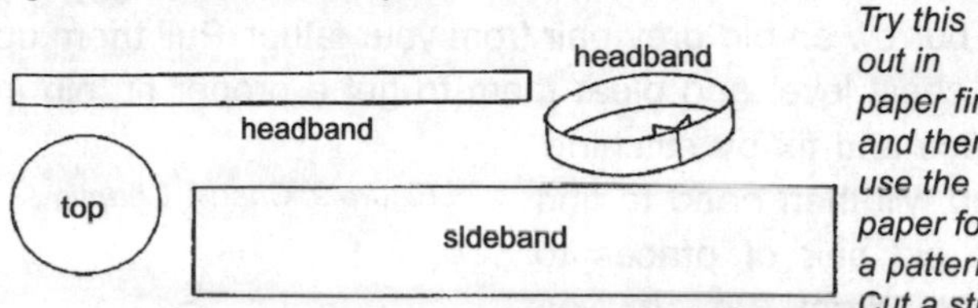

Try this out in paper first and then use the paper for a pattern. Cut a strip of felt about 4 centimetres (1½ inches) wide plus 10 millimetres (½ inch) for the seams by the measurement taken around the your head. Iron on interfacing and join to form a ring to make the headband. Cut a circle of felt about 16 centimetres (6½ inches) in diameter, and a strip of felt about 13 centimetres (6½ inches) deep by the length of the first band plus a quarter of this length plus 10 millimetres (½ inch) for seams (sideband). Join the strip sideband to form a circle, gather up the top and bottom of this until it fits the circle on one side and the headband on the other. Lay the circle over the sideband and stitch it down by hand. Bring the headband over the other side and stitch by hand. For the peak, cut the shape illustrated in card, snip the inner edge as shown and slip this under the headband and stitch. Paint the peak black.

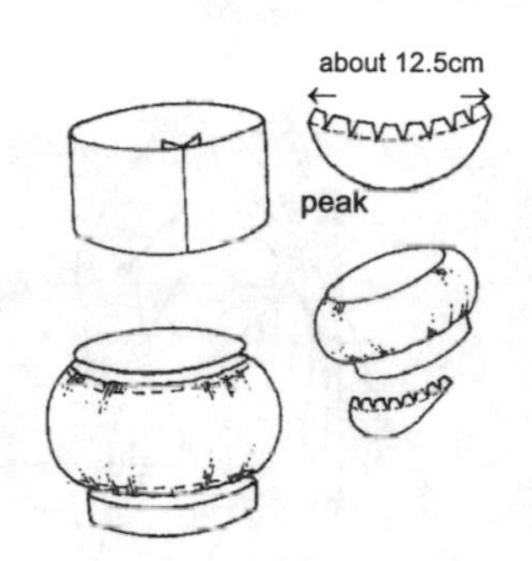

be made in paper or Vilene and attached, and the tie should be striped. If you cannot borrow a suitable tie you can make one out of some old striped fabric.

The trousers should be very oversize and baggy. Try to borrow an old grey pair from your father. Pull them up to chest level and pleat them to get a proper fit; pin in place and fix by stitching. You will then need to find an old pair of braces to keep them up. If you cannot find braces, then attach lengths of elastic that will go over your shoulders.

Figure 9: Charlie Chaplin

Try to borrow a black bowler hat and pad the inside to make it fit. If you cannot find one then you should be able to buy a cheap imitation in a toy or a joke shop.

The costume will not be complete without the walking cane and the moustache, which can be drawn on with a black eyebrow pencil.

PART THREE

ECONOMY COSTUMES

The next group of costumes can be made from cheap materials, and they are fairly easy to make, although you will probably need some help with the fitting.

Project

Fairy and Columbine

For both costumes (*see* figure 10) find the pattern for a tight-fitting bodice with a point at the front. Cut it out in any old fabric (an old sheet will do), tack it up and ask an adult to fit it, making it tight. Mark the fitting lines carefully and take it apart. This bodice can be used as the lining.

Place the sections of the fitted bodice on to the new fabric you are using. If you can find a remnant of a shiny satin-look material this would be very nice. Cut out, tack the two fabrics together on the fitting lines, and make up as one fabric.

The bodice will need to be 'boned' on all the seams and the neck, bottom edge and armholes should be faced (*see* figure 11). Fasten with an open-ended zipper down the back, using to the manufacturer's instructions.

For the skirt of both costumes you need three or four layers of a stiffer material like organza or tarlatan or, if you have a little more money, make the top layers in net.

Figure 10: Fairy and Columbine

Fairy *Columbine*

Put four yards by the length in the first layer and five yards by the length in the top layer. To avoid seams, cut the fabric lengthways. Machine up the seam in each layer, leaving about 15 centimetres (6 inches) for an opening. Gather each section up until it measures the

Figure 11: Boning the bodice and making the wings

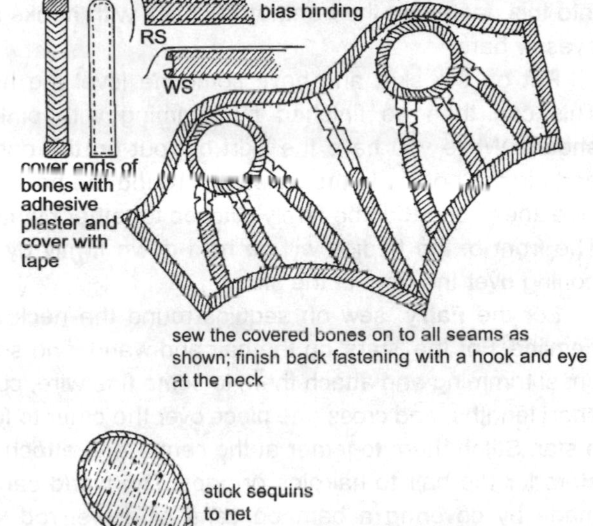

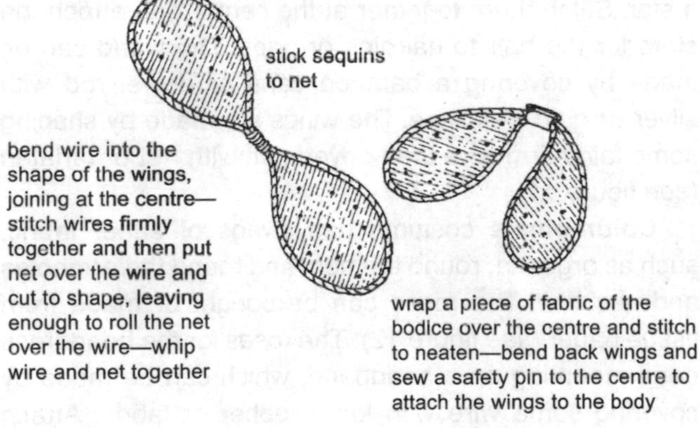

same as your waist. Tack the three or four layers together. Make a waistband and insert the layers of skirt into this, fastening the band at the back with hooks and eyes or bars.

Put on the skirt and have someone level the hem. This can then be finished by trimming with pinking shears. While you have the skirt on, put on the bodice and pin the bodice to the waistband round the back and side; these can then be firmly stitched together by hand. The front of the bodice will be held down firmly by the boning over the front of the skirt.

For the **Fairy**, sew on sequins round the neck and hemline. For the 'stars' on the hair and wand, find some tinsel trimming and attach them to some fine wire, cut in short lengths, and cross one piece over the other to form a star. Stitch them together at the centre and attach the stars for the hair to hairpins or grips. The wand can be made by covering a bamboo cane or dowel rod with silver or gold Sellotape. The wings are made by shaping some fairly firm wire then covering it with net or tarlatan (*see* figure 11).

Columbine's costume has swags of sheer fabric, such as organza, round the hem and round the armholes and neckline. The roses can be bought or made from tissue paper (*see* figure 12). The roses for the headdress need mounting on a headband, which can be made by covering some wire with foam rubber or fabric. Attach two small combs to the band to help hold it in position on the head. The fairy costume is white, with silver or gold sequins, wand and stars. Columbine can be pink or white, with trimming roses.

Project

Make Columbine roses

Cut a piece of pink tissue paper 25 centimetres (10 inches) square and fold it four times, as shown in figure 12.

Cut the petal shapes as shown at A. Unfold the tissue and you will find you have four sets of petal pieces, as in

Figure 12: Making Columbine's roses from tissue paper

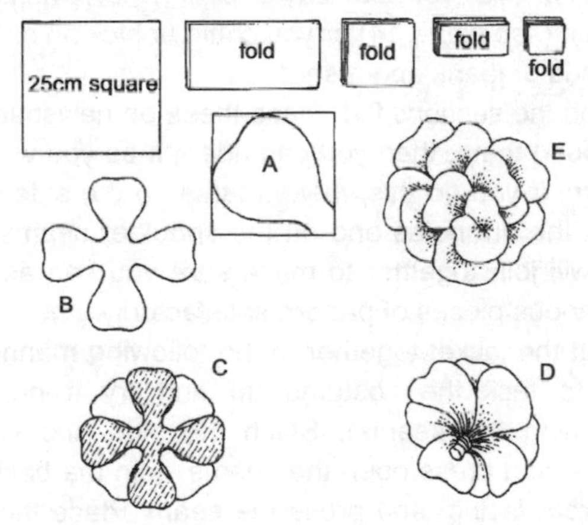

B. With a little dab of glue place the petal pieces one over the other (*see* C). Squeeze the pasted part together and twist slightly to strengthen; wind a thread or Sellotape around this piece and arrange the petals (*see* D and E). Attach them to the dress and headband.

Project

Enter the clown

You can make this clown costume (*see* figure 13) from sheeting or curtain lining material, or cut up an old sheet. But *first* you will need to make a pattern for the jacket and trousers.

To do this, you can buy a pattern for pyjamas and adapt it (*see* figure 14) or you could unpick an old pair of pyjamas or jeans and a shirt.

Iron the sections flat. Place these on newspaper and cut round them, then you can adapt it as you would the pattern. If you do this, make marks on the side seams, round the armholes and on the shoulder seams where they will join together to make sure you can assemble the various pieces of pattern satisfactorily.

Put the jacket together in the following manner (it is best to tack the costume up and try it on before machining the seams). Stitch the side and shoulder seams, and press open the seams. Join the back, neck and front facing, and press the seam. Place the facing

Figure 13: The clown

over the garment, right sides facing, and machine round the edge. Trim the seam, 'clipping in' round the neck and across the corners. Turn facing to the inside and tack round the edge, rolling the seam slightly to the inside, and press.

Machine up the sleeve seams and hem around the bottom edge. Insert the sleeves into the armholes and

Figure 14: Adapting a pyjama jacket

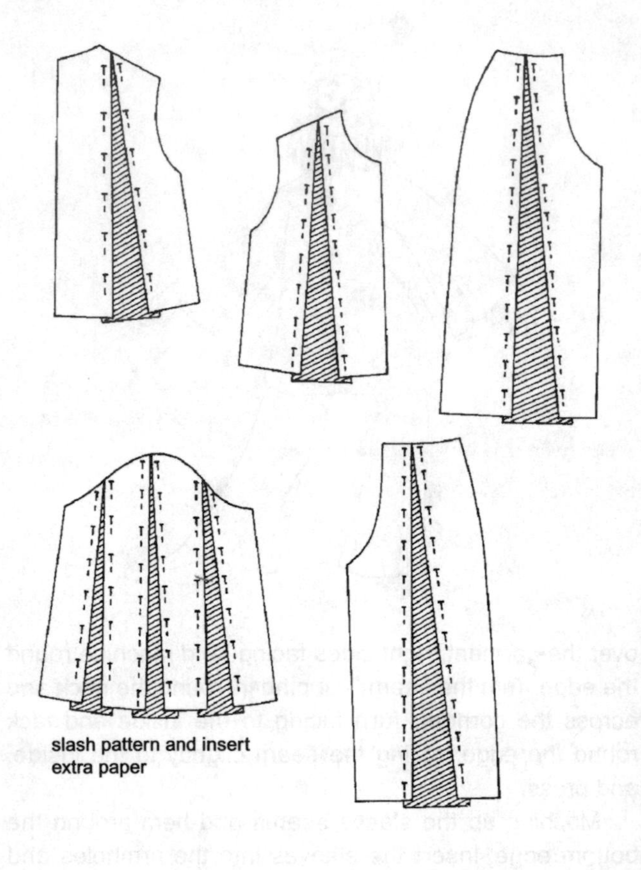

machine. Press seam away from the armhole. Hem the bottom of the jacket, sew on press fasteners to fasten the front—use big ones and place them so the 'pompoms' may be sewn over them.

Stitch the trousers together as follows (it will be easier to put a zip fastener at the side than to attempt a fly opening). Stitch the side seams and inside leg seams first, leaving about 18–20 centimetres (7–8 inches) on the left side for the zip. Join the leg pieces together round the crutch. Hem the bottoms. Insert the zip. Make a waistband to fit your waist plus 5 centimetres (2 inches) overlap, and insert the waist of the trousers into it; let the 5 centimetres (2 inches) extend on the underside of the wrap; fasten with hooks and eyes or bars. Add 'pompoms'.

Project

Make a ruff—pompoms and skull cap

You will need nylon organza to make the ruff (*see* instructions and figures 15 and 16), knitting wool to make the pompoms and an old white sock or stocking to make the skull cap. Art felt can be used to make the hat.

Make-up

Traditional make-up for the stage is oil-based and is relatively messy to apply and remove compared with the range of nontoxic, water-based face paints available

Figure 15: Stand-up collars—the ruff

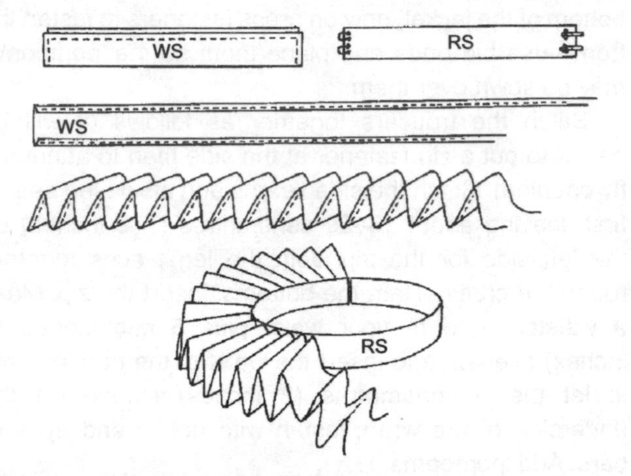

First make a neckband of soft white cotton (poplin or lawn will do) 7.5 centimetres (3 inches) plus 2 centimetres (3/4 inch) for the seams, by your neck measurement (not too tight), plus 2 centimetres (3/4 inch) for seams. Fold and machine as shown leaving a small section unstitched for turning. Trim the seams and corners and turn to right side and press. Slip-stitch the open section together and attach hooks and eyes for fastening. Take a long strip of organza, at least four times the length of your neckband (join as necessary), by 7.5 centimetres (3 inches) to 10 centimetres (4 inches) plus 10 millimetres (1/2 inch) for turnings, turn in the 5 millimetres (1/4 inch) either side and machine. With a tape measure handy and an iron, press the strip into pleats 4 centimetres (1 1/2 inch) deep. Then sew the top and bottom of the inner edge of the pleats to the neckband, spreading the pleats out slightly as you do so. It is easiest to sew the top edge first and the lower edge second. The spacing is important—not too close and not too wide.

Figure 16: The clown's hat

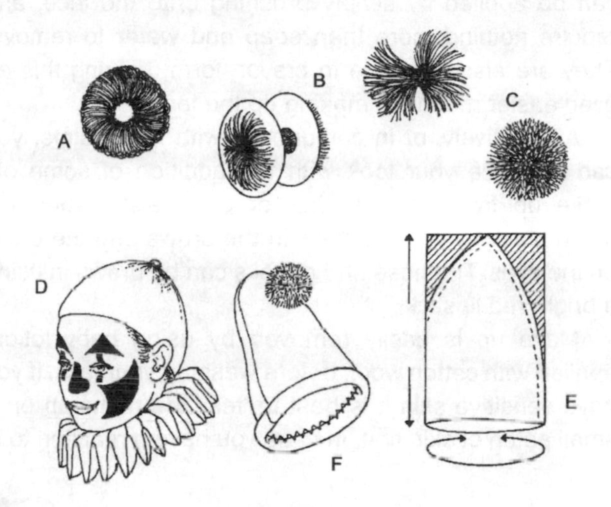

Pompoms: Cut two circles of card about 5 centimetres (2 inches) in diameter with a hole in the middle place them together and wind thick wool through the hole and over the outside. When completely covered (A), cut through the centre outer edge and pull the cards apart (B); wind wool around the centre, pull tight and secure (C). Fluff out the pompom.

Skull cap: Pull the top of a stocking over your head, pull the top together and cut off the surplus. Secure the top by stitching (D).

Cap: Make a paper pattern first; fold a sheet in half and cut a shape as illustrated (E); pin and try on. If satisfactory, cut up felt and stitch seam as shown. Press open and turn to wrong side; strengthen the edge by stitching on a strip of felt for a facing; catch-stitch in place. Sew on the pompoms (F).

from any fancy dress shop or toy retailer. Face paints can be applied by simply brushing onto the face, and require nothing more than soap and water to remove. They are also available in crayon form, making this an even easier means of making up the face.

Alternatively, or in conjunction with face paints, you can enhance your look with the addition of some old make up from your mother or elder sister—perhaps some black eyeliner to draw in the brows and the cross on the eyes. The nose and cheeks can be drawn in using a bright red lipstick.

Make up is easily removed by using baby lotion, applied with cotton wool, before washing your face. If you have sensitive skin it is best to 'test' the make-up on a small patch of skin first, in case you have a reaction to it.

Project

Be a gypsy

This is a costume suitable for girls of any age (*see* figure 17). You will need a blouse made of a fine soft white fabric, such as muslin, gathered into a fairly low neckline and with large gathered sleeves. This is easy to make if you can find a pattern. Or you can make your own pattern by adapting a fitted bodice and sleeve as shown in figure 18 and its instructions.

The bolero is made in felt, which can be obtained by

Figure 17: A gypsy

the metre at haberdashery departments and stores. If you do not want the costume to last long, this can be cut out and just seamed up the neckline, armholes and bottom being 'pinked'. To make it stronger, machine-stitch bias binding round the edges on the wrong side. Interline and face the fronts, and insert eyelets (which can be bought from a haberdashery department) and tie with fine cord or bootlaces.

The choice of colour is up to you, but try to keep it bright—blues, greens and reds look really effective.

The skirt should be very full and gathered from the waistband, with an extra flounce approximately 25–30 centimetres (10–12 inches) deep. The skirt and flounce should be in different printed fabrics that go well together, a small print for the skirt and a large print for the flounce. Again the choice of colour is up to you, but make sure that your colours do not clash with one another.

If you are making a new skirt, cut the material lengthways to avoid having more than one seam; do the same with the flounce. Wear as many petticoats as you can make or borrow; these should be white.

For the headscarf, it is worthwhile ironing on Vilene to the part that goes round your head so it will stand up stiffly. Wear lots of necklaces, wooden beads and gold earrings. Gold hoop earrings are ideal, but if you do not have your ears pierced, then any large gold clip-on earrings will look good.

Complete the costume with a pair of flat, strappy sandals, or go barefoot if it is warm enough to do so.

Figure 18: A gypsy blouse

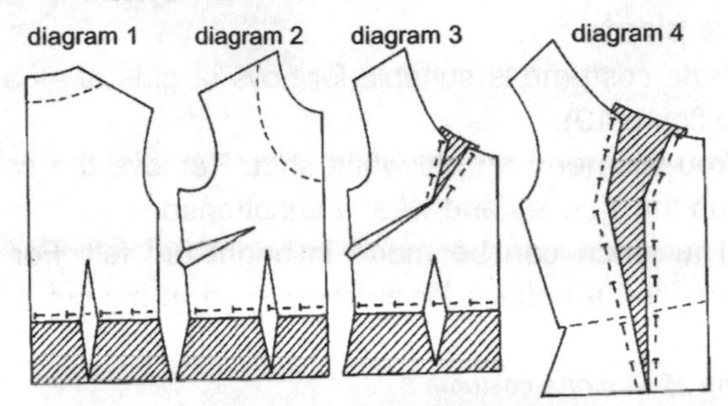

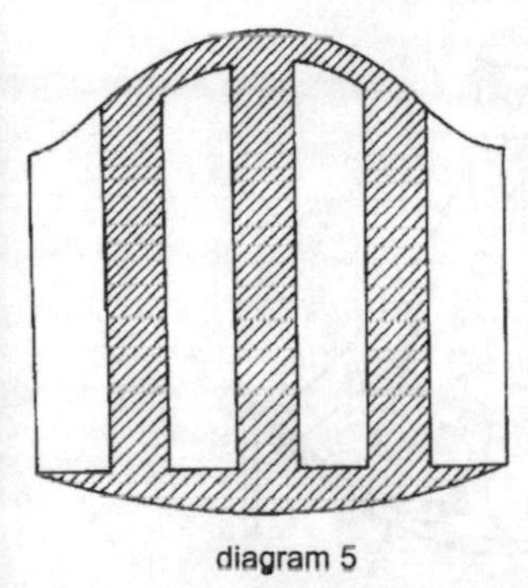

diagram 5

Take a normal fitting bodice and straight sleeve. Lengthen by adding about 12.5 centimetres (5 inches) additional pattern below the waist; continue to dart and shape the side out slightly (measure on yourself for amount)—see diagrams 1 and 2. Slash down from the now neck to the point of the dart; fold dart, opening the neckline; paste paper under (see diagram 3). Slash down again from the neckline to the bottom and open out to give an extra 7.5–10 centimetres (3–4 inches) to gather into the neck (see diagram 4). Slash the sleeve into four equal parts and open out, also increasing the height and the length (see diagram 5). To make up—machine the darts, side, shoulder and sleeve seams; then press. Sew bias binding around neckline and lower edge of sleeves. Insert elastic and draw up required amount, securing the ends of elastic. Insert sleeves into armhole. Hem bottom of blouse.

Be a pirate

A pirate costume is suitable for boys or girls of all ages (*see* figure 19).

You will need an old white shirt. Remove the collar, roll up the sleeves and wear it unbuttoned.

The jerkin can be made in bright red felt. For the shape, find a pattern for a dressing gown but cut it to a

Figure 19: A pirate costume

Figure 20: A pirate hat

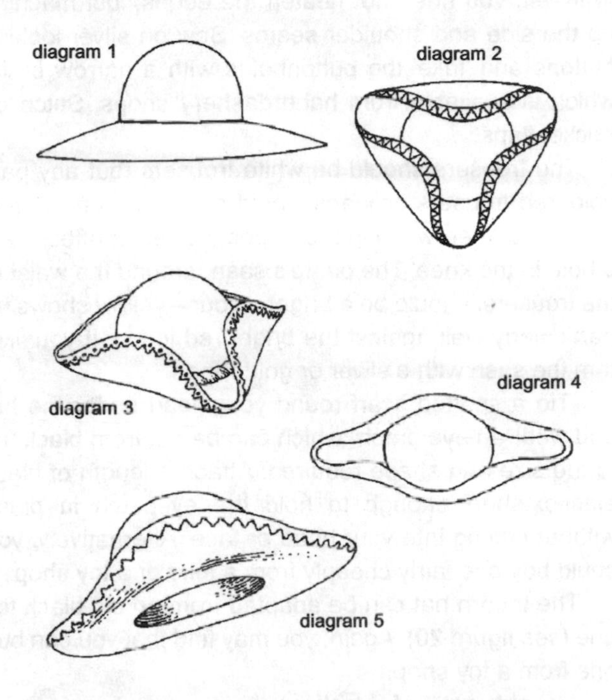

Find a large-brimmed black felt hat like the one in diagram 1. Fold the brim up as shown in diagram 2 and stitch in position and trim the edges with silver or gold gallon or braid. Tie a cord around the crown (diagram 3). An alternative hat is one turned up at the back and front as in diagrams 4 and 5. This would be good trimmed with gold lace. You may be able to find a nylon type that is cheap or you could cut up gold doilies and stick them on.

shorter length and without a collar, lapels or sleeves. With felt, you need not neaten the edges; just machine up the side and shoulder seams. Sew on silver-looking buttons and 'fake' the buttonholes with a narrow braid, which is available from haberdashery shops. Stitch on pocket flaps.

The trousers should be white trousers (but any pale coloured trousers or jeans would do). Cut them off just below the knee with jagged edges. For extra effect, tear a hole in the knee. The pirate's sash, around the waist of the trousers, should be a bright colour—yellow shows up particularly well against the bright red jerkin. If you like, trim the sash with a silver or gold fringe.

Tie a spotted scarf round your head under the hat and wear an eye patch, which can be cut from black felt to the size and shape required. Attach a length of black elastic, short enough to hold the eyepatch in place without cutting into your head or face. Alternatively, you could buy one fairly cheaply from a joke or a toy shop.

The tricorn hat can be adapted from an old black felt one (*see* figure 20). Again, you may find that you can buy one from a toy shop.

An old pair of black wellingtons, folded over at the top, would provide you with ideal boots. To complete your pirate costume, try to find a pair of simple, gold-coloured clip-on earrings.

PART FOUR

DRESS A NATIVITY PLAY

Here are some ideas for the costumes to be used in a Nativity play. A lot of the materials and parts of the costumes may be found around your home, or you can use the fabrics suggested in the descriptions of the costumes, all of which are fairly cheap.

Mary

Mary wears a long-sleeved dress, a long cloak fastened with cord at the front, a wimple and veil, and sandals. It should be easy to borrow the pattern (or your teacher could help you make one) for the dress. It would be unfitted with narrow 'set-in' sleeves and a high neck. As it will not show, it could be fastened with a zip at the back. The dress would be made in fine wool or fairly thick cotton, in cream or pale blue (an old winceyette sheet would do).

The cloak can be cut as shown in figure 22, preferably in a clear blue felt. A heavy curtaining would do, but in this case you would have to neaten the edges; with felt it can be left as cut.

Project

Make Mary's veil

Use a fine white cotton lawn or an old net curtain. *See*

figure 23 for instructions on making the veil and the wimple. As a little detail, add one or two lines of braid on the hem of the dress and at the end of the veil—they should be in a matching or a slightly deeper-toned colour.

Figure 21: Mary and Joseph

Figure 22: Cut your own pattern for Mary's cloak

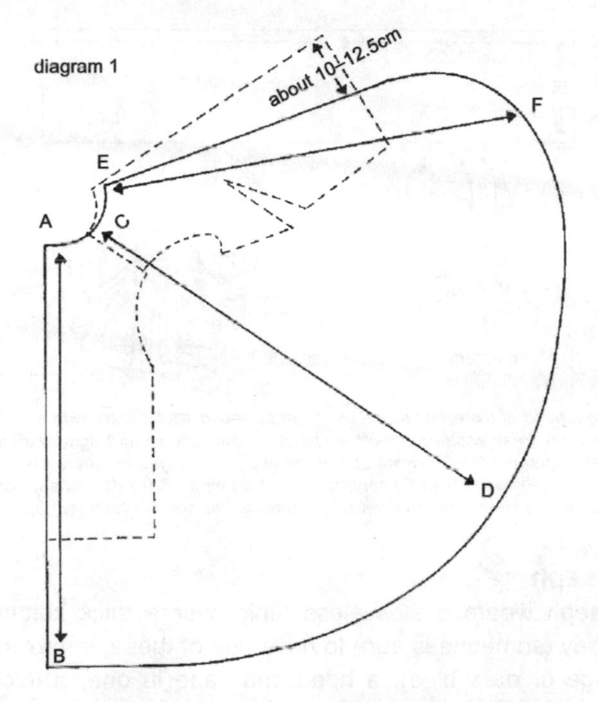

To make the pattern, place both sides of a simple blouse with the shoulders together. Measure A B, the length from nape to ground plus 5 centimetres (2 inches); C D, from neck over the shoulder to ground plus 2.5 centimetres (1 inch) and E F from front neck to ground. Trace the hem and between these points. With 1.8 metre (72 inches) wide fabric it may be possible to cut the cloak with a fold at the back. Otherwise put a seam here. With narrow fabric you may need to make a join.

Figure 23: Mary's veil and wimple

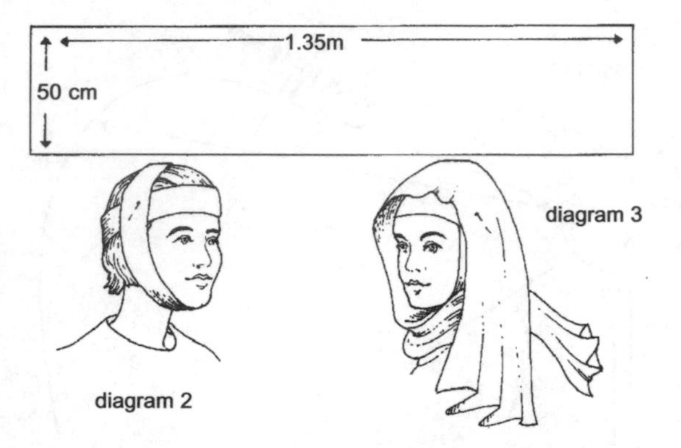

Take a band of material around the head as shown and secure with a safety pin. Pass another under the chin as shown and secure again with a safety pin at the top (diagram 2). Pin the two bands together where they cross. Cut the veil about 50 centimetres x 1.35 metre (20 x 42 inches) and drape it as shown. Secure it with a pin through the wimple (diagram 3).

Joseph

Joseph wears a sleeveless tunic over a thick knitted jersey (someone is sure to have one of these, in brown, beige or dark blue), a hood and cape in one, a thick leather belt and pouch, and sandals. He carries a staff and blanket. The tunic can be made of wool or felt, any brownish colour, and the pattern for a pyjama jacket can be adapted for use. It needs no fastening as the neck can be cut wide enough to pull over the head. You should

Figure 24: Joseph's pouch

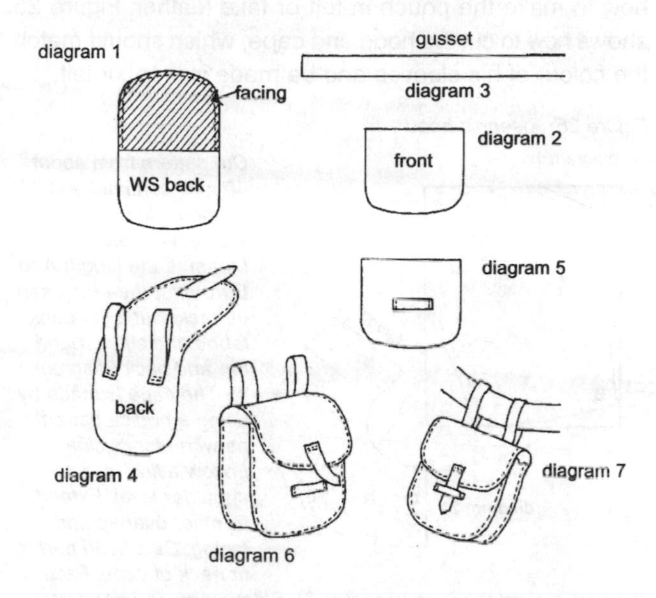

Cut the back of the pouch about 2 x 2.5 centimetres (3/4 x 1 inch). Face the flap and stitch around on the right side (diagram 1). Cut the front about 2 x 2 centimetres (3/4 x 3/4 inch) ; cut the gusset 4 centimetres (1 1/2 inch) x the length around the two sides and the bottom of the front (diagrams 2 and 3). Make loops for attaching the pouch to the belt and the tab for fastening. Sew these onto the back of the pouch and a bar for fastening onto the front. Join the back to the front (diagram 6). Pleat the gusset at the top and stitch firmly. Slip the belt through the loops (diagram 7).

be able to borrow a thick belt, and figure 24 shows you how to make the pouch in felt or fake leather. Figure 25 shows how to cut the hood and cape, which should match the colour of his sleeves and be made in wool or felt.

Figure 25: Joseph's hood

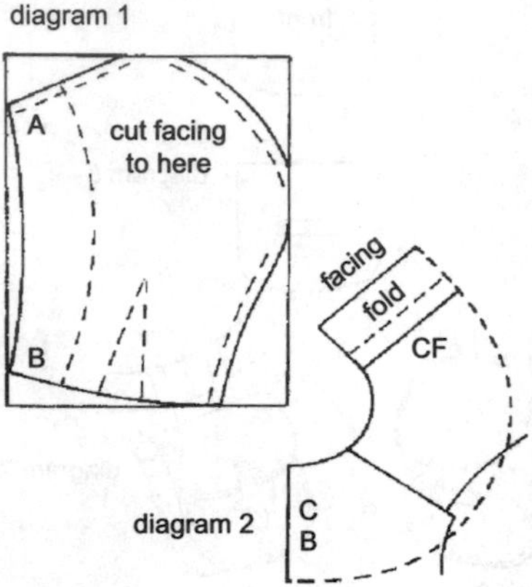

Cut pattern from about 40 x 30 centimetre (17 X 12 inch) cloth, then shape as shown. Measure the length A to B from forehead to base of neck. Cut it in double fabric and stitch round top and back (diagram 1). The cape is made by using a bodice pattern, as with Mary's cloak. Follow a line round at shoulder level. Extend front for overlap and facing. Dart head part to fit neck of cape. Face the part around the face (diagram 2). Stitch cape and head part together.

Project

Be an angel

The whole of this costume (*see* figure 26) could be made in Vilene, but if you already have a white dress that is very plain and long this would do for the underdress.

Figure 26: An angel's costume with cloak

The wings are really a cloak, cut as in figure 27 and covered with feathers cut from Vilene, paper or felt, which can be stuck on the base.

The angel's cloak is styled very like Mary's but cut

away more at the front and not curved at the bottom. 'Layer' the 'feathers', making them larger as you get to the bottom and spread them out more.

Figure 27: Grading the layers of feathers on a cloak

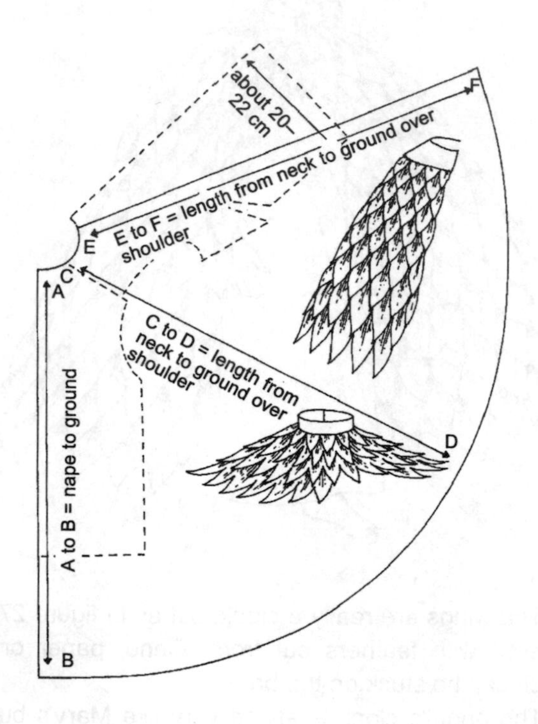

Make an angel's cape

There is also a cape, which is treated in the same way as the cloak plus long feathers over the shoulders. This is attached to a high collar and it is fastened at the back. Place a bodice pattern together as shown in diagram 1 for the pattern of the cape (*see* figure 28). Cut a collar pattern about 7.5 centimetres (3 inches) plus 1 centimetre (½ inch) for the seams by the neck measurements, fold it in half and machine the ends; snip the seams and trim to the right side. To attach the collar to the cape, place the collar, right sides facing, to the cape neck and machine round. Turn the collar over, turn in the seam allowance and slip hem on to the machine stitching, as in diagrams 2–6 of figure 28. Attach the feathers. Fasten at the neck with hooks and eyes.

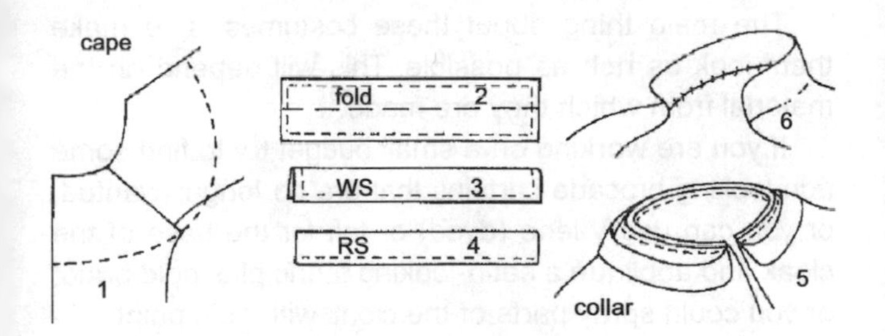

Figure 28: Angel's cape

You might like to keep the costume all gold and white, in which case spray the whole cloak and the cape with gold paint. You can buy aerosol spray paint from hardware and stationery shops, but always ensure that you use the spray in a well-ventilated room away from direct heat and naked flames. Otherwise you can use some light brown felt in amongst the other feathers. It would also be nice to add a few real little fluffy feathers here and there.

Project

Kings' costume

Nativity plays sometimes present the Magi as three wise men and sometimes as the three kings—so here are costumes that, with a change of headdress, can suggest either. They consist of a cloak fastened with large press fasteners under the buttons, plus, for the king, a crown and wide collar, and for a wise man a draped headdress (*see* figure 29).

The main thing about these costumes is to make them look as rich as possible. This will depend on the material from which they are made.

If you are working on a small budget try to find some rich-looking brocade curtains that are no longer wanted, or you can use Vilene (dyed) or felt for the base of the cloak and appliqué a satin-looking fabric plus gold braid; or you could spray parts of the cloak with gold paint.

Figure 29: The King's costume and the draped headdress of the Wise man

Experiment a little to see what effect you can obtain, remembering that the garment will be seen from a distance. Spraying gold paint through paper doilies can give a very good effect.

The cape would look very rich made of gold stretch leather cloth (obtainable from specialist stockists) plus the addition of gold-sprayed straws or thick braid. As an alternative to the cape, you could use several gilt chains or chain belts. Fix them on the shoulders away from the neck so that they hang a little way down the back, and do not move around.

The king's crown is made from a very fine wire mesh For the decoration you can use drinking straws stuck in place and then sprayed gold (*see* figure 33 on page 59).

The wise man's headdress is very simple—just a cloth over the head, bound round with another piece of material. Keep the colours rich—deep blues, crimson, ochre yellow and gold. These men were said to come from the East, so look at any books you can find illustrating Eastern art and crafts, including fabrics, to help you choose colours.

Project

King's cloak

Place a blouse or shirt pattern shoulder to shoulder as shown (*see* figure 30), and measure length to obtain a pattern—allow for wrap and facing at the front. If using

Figure 30: The pattern for the king's cloak

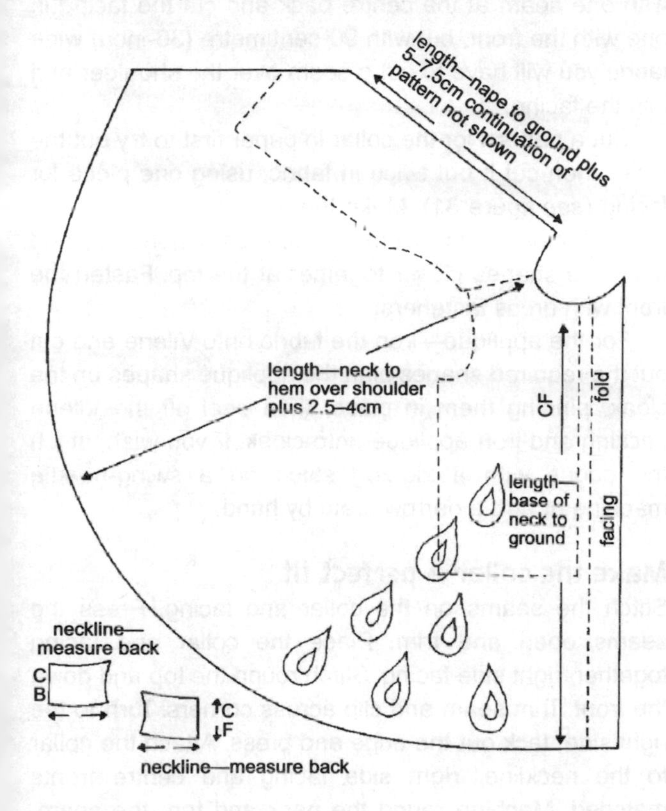

very wide fabric (1.8 metres/72 inches) you can manage with one seam at the centre back and cut the facing in one with the front, but with 90-centimetre (36-inch) wide fabric you will have to put a seam over the shoulder and join the facing.

Cut a pattern for the collar in paper first to try out the size—then cut it out twice in fabric, using one piece for facing (*see* figure 31). Make the appliqué pattern larger at the bottom of the cloak, smaller as it goes up, and bring the shapes closer together at the top. Fasten the front with press fasteners.

For the appliqué—iron the fabric onto Vilene and cut out the required shapes plan the appliqué shapes on the cloak, pinning them in place, then peel off the Vilene backing and iron appliqué onto cloak. If you wish, stitch the edges with a zig-zag stitch on a swing-needle machine or add a narrow braid by hand.

Make the collar a perfect fit

Stitch the seams on the collar and facing. Press the seams open and trim. Place the collar and facing together, right side facing. Stitch round the top and down the front. Trim seam and clip across corners. Turn to the right side, tack out the edge and press. Attach the collar to the neckline, right side facing and centre fronts matched. Machine round the neck and trim the seam. Turn the collar seam allowance under on the wrong side and hem to machine stitching. Fasten with hooks and eyes.

Figure 31

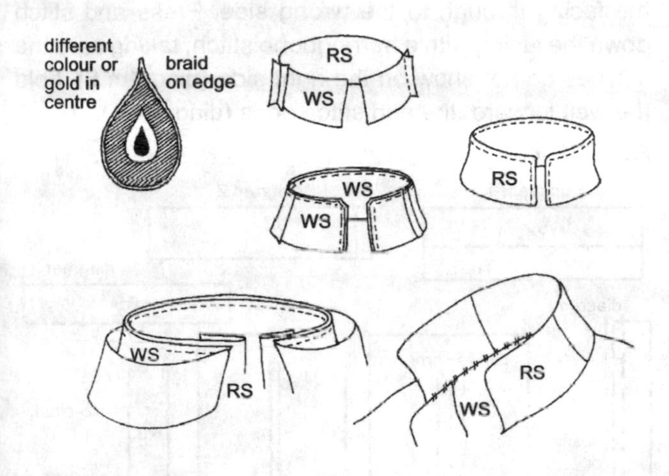

Invisible facing

To create the openings for the hands, put the cloak on and mark the positions where it is convenient to put your hands through. Cut a strip of fabric for a welt, the length of the opening plus seams by about 7.5 centimetres (3 inches), as in diagram 1 in figure 32. Fold in half and stitch ends; snip and trim seams; turn to the right side and press (diagrams 2 and 3). Place welt against the position of the opening, raw edges to the front. Place a facing over this, right sides facing, tack and stitch round as shown in diagram 5 of figure 32. Slash through between the stitching, snipping into the corners, and pull the facing through to the wrong side. Press and stitch down the facing with a herringbone stitch, taking care the stitches do not show on the right side (diagram 6). Fold the welt forward, the and stitch ends (diagram 7).

Figure 32: Invisible facings

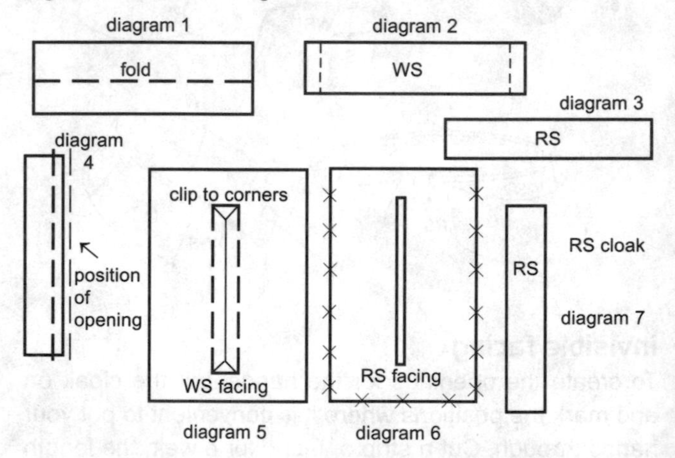

Making and decorating the crown and collar

For the crown, cut a bias strip of fine wire mesh 7–7.5 centimetres (2½–3 inches) by your head measurements (*see* diagram 1 of figure 33). Make a join on the straight, folding back the mesh covering and wrapping one side over the other. Whip-stitch mesh wire around the lower edge (diagram 2). Damp the mesh and shape the crown wider at the top, then wire this edge (diagram 3). Stick drinking straws to the mesh base and stitch a band by hand around the head fitting. Make this in fake gold leather if possible (diagram 4). Spray the whole thing with gold paint and, if you wish, add fake jewels between some of the straws.

Use the same collar as shown in figure 28. Stick on straws and jewels, if wanted, and bind the neck by hand. Fasten with hooks and eyes, sewn on the wrong side (diagram 5).

Figure 33: The crown and collar

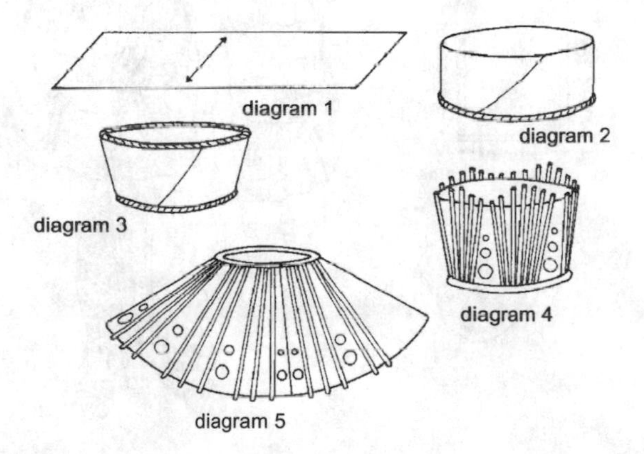

Dress shepherds

These shepherds' costumes (figure 34) can be made from all kinds of odds and ends—old blankets, sheets and bedcovers, some dyed. Old pyjamas or jeans will make the trousers, just as long as the materials look home-made, as the shepherds were peasant people who would weave their own fabrics.

The first shepherd wears clothes very like Joseph's

Figure 34: Shepherd boys

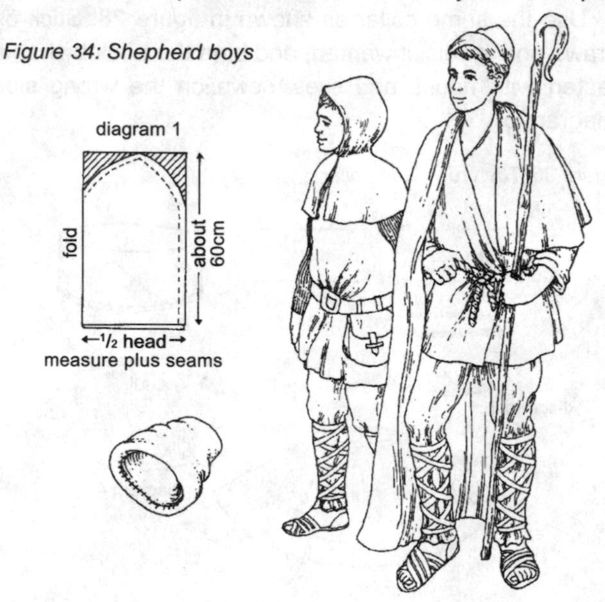

and the same patterns could be used for the tunic (although cut shorter), the hood and cape, and the belt and pouch.

The trousers are bound close to the leg from below the knee. Old strips of woollen cloth could be used for this, or the woollen braid you can buy at most stores at the haberdashery or trimming counter.

The second shepherd wears a soft cap cut in jersey, rather like the clown's and then crushed down. A judo top, if you can borrow one, would be ideal for the wrap-around coat. It is tied at the waist with a thick cord. The trousers are the same as for the first shepherd. Throw a small coarse blanket or piece of fabric over the shoulders. Both wear very simple sandals.

All the shepherds could wear a variation of these costumes, making some long, and perhaps using a cloak or cape with hood attached. Keep all the colours in the brown-cream range with just a touch of blue or orangy red.

When planning the colours of the play, cut little patterns of the fabrics and look at them in groups as the characters appear. Try to obtain some exciting effects: rich vivid colours and gold for the Magi; blue and cream or white and gold for Mary and the angels—then simple earthy colours for the shepherds. Remember that texture is almost as important as colour.

PART FIVE

FORMING A BASIC WARDROBE

If you are helping to run a drama group or you are working on the costumes for drama productions at school, it is a good idea to build up gradually, as your finances allow, a group of these costumes.

They should be made in wool preferably, but some cotton or dull rayon upholstery fabrics might do. Use strong fabric that 'hangs' well, and buy 1.35-metre (54-inch) or 1.2-metre (48-inch) wide fabric, as this will prove more economical.

The colours are best kept fairly 'earthy'—avoid acid colours, which were developed later, so that the costumes will 'fit in' with a greater number of plays.

These costumes will prove extremely useful for most characters, except those that have to be very rich or if the costume has to be very elaborate.

If you make costumes that are very definitely of one period you will find them far less useful than one that, with the addition of a few 'bits and pieces', will suggest the period.

For girls the basic costume consists of a plain bodice with a high neck and long tight-fitting sleeves, and fastens at the back with hooks and eyes; plus two half-circular full-length 'skirts' with press fasteners down the

Figure 35: A girl's basic costume

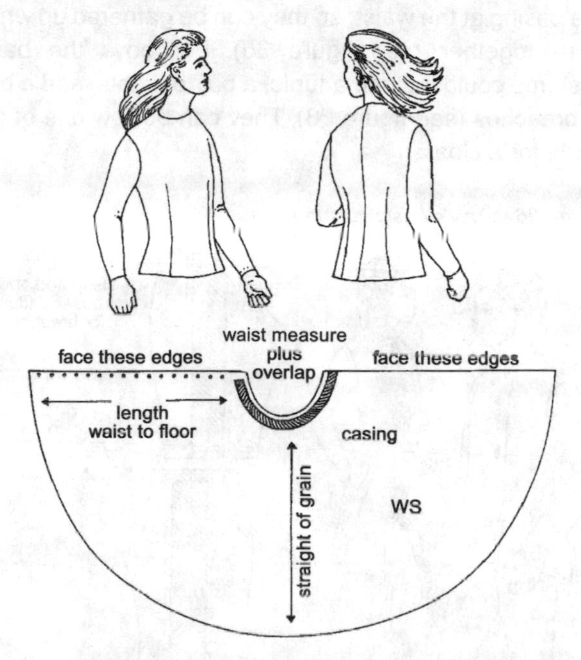

You can probably find a pattern which is as simple as the sketch. Make it up according to the directions, but do put a fastening with hooks and eyes down the back. Keep the sleeves just wide enough to put your hand through, avoiding an opening. Cut the skirt as in the diagram face the edges; turn in the waist edge about 5 millimetres (1/4 inch), and stitch a strip (cut on the bias) of fabric to form a casing, turning in the edges and machining. Turn up hem and slipstitch in place.

seam so they can be worn separately or together—there is a casing at the waist, so they can be gathered up when worn together (*see* figure 35). For boys the basic costume could include a tunic, a pair of tights, and a pair of breeches (see figure 36). They can borrow one of the skirts for a cloak.

Figure 36: A boy's basic costume

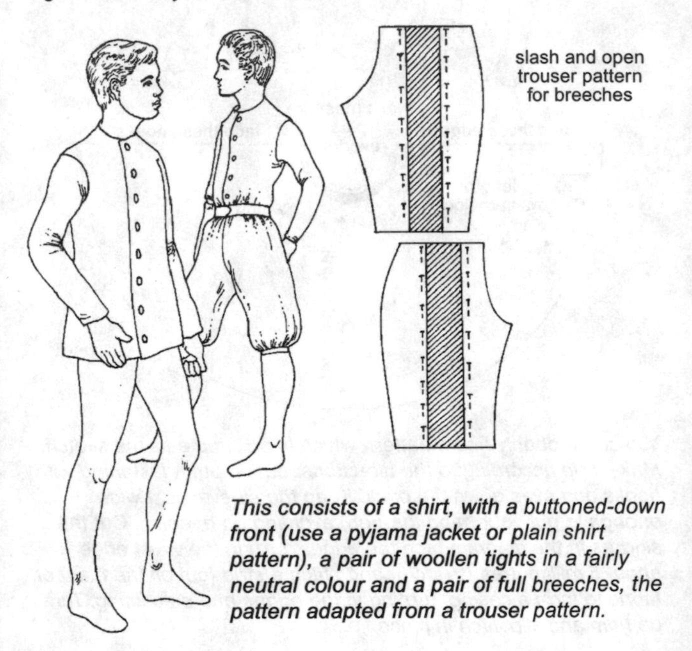

This consists of a shirt, with a buttoned-down front (use a pyjama jacket or plain shirt pattern), a pair of woollen tights in a fairly neutral colour and a pair of full breeches, the pattern adapted from a trouser pattern.

For girls

Go medieval by using the basic bodice and one skirt add; a headdress like Mary's and a belt and pouch like Joseph's (*see* previous projects). The other skirt is worn as a cloak. Add an underskirt or petticoat if possible (*see* figure 37).

Figure 37: Girl's medieval costume

Figure 38: Girl's Elizabethan costume

Be Elizabethan (*see* figure 38). Use the bodice and the two skirts (press-stud the skirts together and pull a cord through the casing to fit the waist). Add bands on the skirt, a sleeveless jerkin (figure 39), an organza or lawn cap (figure 40), a ruff (like the clown's) and cuffs.

Figure 39: A sleeveless jerkin

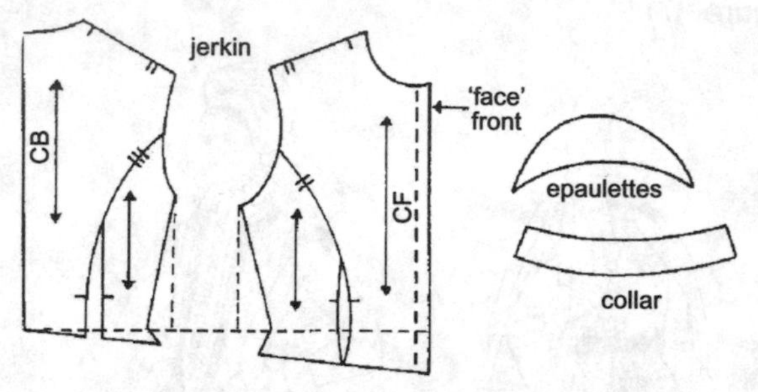

Made the jerkin in felt or woollen cloth, based on a bodice, cut to a point in the front with a hook and bar fastening (buttons sewn on top). Cut epaulettes in double material and interline—shape as indicated (measure armhole for length). Stitch outer edge, trim seam, turn and press. Sew to armhole by hand. Make and attach collar as for king's costume. Attach braid to fronts and epaulettes by hand or machine.

Make a cap

For the Elizabethan cap, make a double band for the front, shaped as shown in figure 40; cut a circle for the

Figure 40: An Elizabethan cap

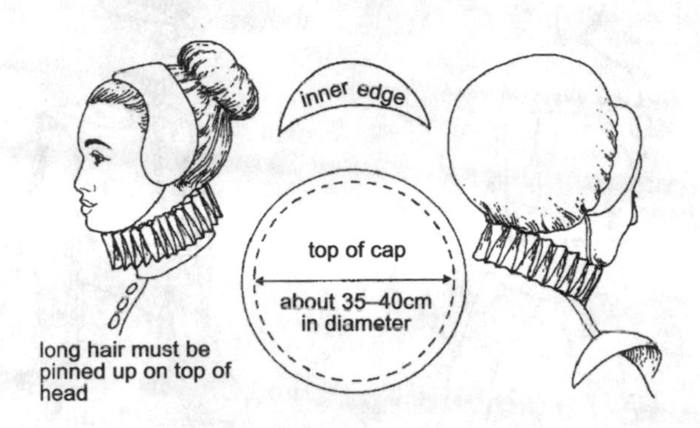

back, gathering it into the band and putting elastic in the turning to hold the back. A little elastic under the chin holds the cap in place. Try it out in paper or old fabric first.

For boys

Go medieval (*see* figure 41). Add a belt and pouch and a hood made like Joseph's.

Be Elizabethan (*see* figure 42). Add to the shirt tights and breeches, a sleeveless jerkin with high collar and epaulettes (base this on a jacket pattern, making it similar to the girl's, but adding a basque), neck and wrist ruffs (as the clown's). One of the spare skirts serves as a cloak and the hat is trimmed with a feather).

Figure 41: Boy's medieval costume

Figure 42: Boy's Elizabethan costume